The mission of Storey Publishing is to serve our customers
by publishing practical information that encourages personal independence
in harmony with the environment.

Edited by Deborah Balmuth
Art direction by Meredith Maker
Text production by Jennifer Jepson Smith
Copyright © 2003 by Deb Koffman

   The information in this book is true and complete to the best of our knowl-
edge. All recommendations are made without guarantee on the part of the
author or Storey Publishing. The author and publisher disclaim any liability in
connection with the use of this information. For additional information please
contact Storey Books, 210 MASS MoCA Way, North Adams, MA 01247.
   Storey books are available for special premium and promotional uses and
for customized editions. For further information, please call Storey's Custom
Publishing Department at 1-800-793-9396.

This book is printed with soy-based inks on recycled paper.

Printed in China by Regent Publishing Services

10 9 8 7 6 5 4 3 2 1

Library of Congress Cataloging-in-Publication Data

Koffman, Deb.
      The Soul Support Book / Deb Koffman
            p.   cm.
      ISBN 1-58017-286-5 (alk. paper)
      1. Conduct of life — Quotations, maxims, etc.   I. Title.

      BJ1581.2 .K64 2003
      170'.44—dc21   2002191137

The SOUL SUPPORT BOOK

By Deb Koffman

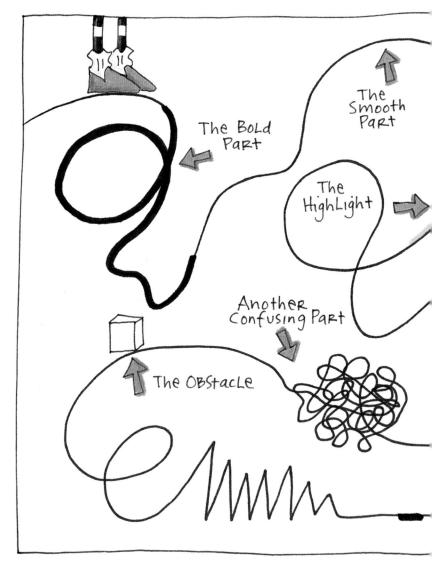

The Smooth Part

The BOLD Part

The HighLight

Another Confusing Part

The OBStacle

MAP of th

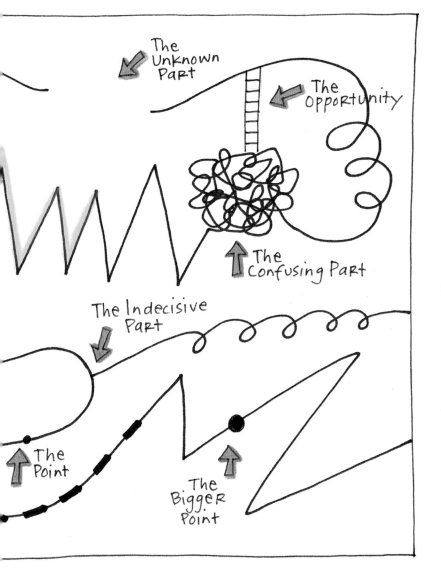

The Unknown Part

The Opportunity

The Confusing Part

The Indecisive Part

The Point

The Bigger Point

TERRITORY

Acknowledgments

To the many friends, teachers, Healers And Books that have Supported my Soul... my deepest gratitude for whatever Led me to your Wisdom.

To Storey Publishing... Deborah, Janet, Pam... for having the Courage to take a Risk on an unknown Artist... for Believing in me and my Work.

To my mother, whose encouragement and wholehearted enthusiasm for my Art nourishes my creative Spirit.

To my Women's <u>Authentic Movement</u> Group... for your unconditional Love and Support. For the Space we Hold for each other's Well-Being, personal Growth and Empowerment.

This Book is dedicated to Sam, Harry, Abe, Isaac, Genevieve and Billie... May you Always Listen to your Heart and follow what Supports your Soul.

DISCOVER YOUR
OWN MEDICINE.

THERE'S ALWAYS ANOTHER
WAY.

INTRODUCTION

THIS Book IS about getting UNStuck.
In YOUR CReative PROjects, YOUR Job,
YOUR RELationShips, YOUR LiFe.

It's ABOut making where you ARe
and what's Happening OK. It's
ABOut THinking in A New way.

It's ABOut getting A BROadeR
View. It's about AcknowLedging
what is TRue.

When you don't know what TO DO,
WHeRe to GO OR what to SAY...

ContempLating these caRtoons
may inspiRe you to PLAY...
in YOUR OWN UNIQUe way.

THIS Book can Be Read. Seen.
in any ORDER. OR You can
RandomLY peRuse.

Any page can be Tasted. FeLt.
As often as You CHoose.

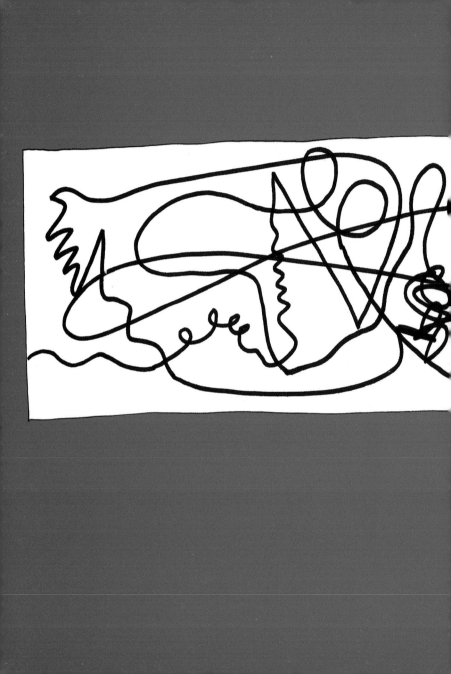

FOLLOW YOUR Intuition.

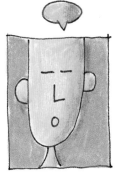

Speak A
Little

Speak A
LOT

Speak
Loudly

Speak
Not

Sometimes
the words are
Down too Deep
To Reach.

When there Are No words...
Something Else WILL Appear.

HATE IT.

USE IT.

AVOID IT.

FACE IT.

FACE IT IN AN Interesting WAY

FACE IT FROM A DIFFERENT Side.

Speak to it.

Listen to it.

Go inside it.

Go beyond it.

See it as a Gift.

See it as a Mystery.

There are many ways to respond to the same thing.

Search for A Resourceful State.

see what
you wish...

See what
you fear.

See what
You THINK...

See what
IS CLEAR.

My Empty
Mind.

My Mind
Filled with IT.

My Mind
Giving Space
To IT.

Don't THINK ABOUT IT.

My Mind STRaining To Understand IT.

My Mind TRYing to Resist IT.

Letting GO of It.

Watch your mind.

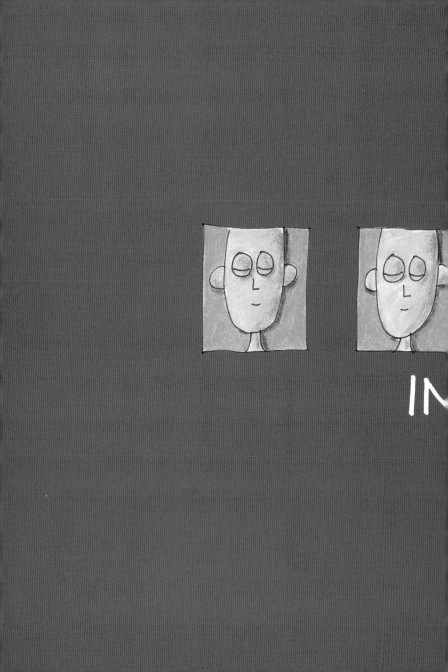

SIGHT.

Open to Something New.

It's NOT what it is...
It's what it INSPIRES
In you.

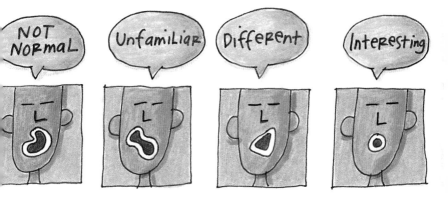

Be Genuinely Curious.

In the Past   In a Littl

Recently

2 Months Ago

yesterday

Next Time

In a year

In a minute

Someday

3 years Ago   Soo.

hiLe
EFORE
TOMORROW
LATER
Next Week
ONCE
Then
In the Future
WHEN
10 years from Now
SHORTLY
LASt week

Notice what is Happening.

THIS IS the PLACE I fell APart

THIS IS the PLACe I found

THIS IS the PLACe I CReated

THIS IS the PLACe I GRound.

THIS IS the PLACE I Came from

THIS IS the PLACe I Denied

THIS IS the PLACe that SCARes me

THIS IS the PLACe I Hide.

THIS IS the PLACE I Remembered

THIS IS the PLACE I FORgot

THIS IS the PLace that BoRes me

THIS IS the PLace I Fought.

THIS IS the PLACE I Danced in

THIS IS the PLACE I WISH FOR

THIS IS the PLace my HeaRt opened

THIS IS the PLace WORth LiVing MoRe.

Appreciate youR Experience.

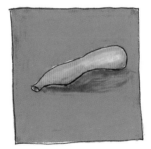

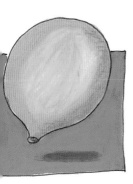
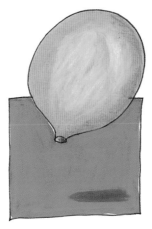

Concentrate on
YOUR Breathing.

Being

Being with STRENGTHS

Being with Weaknesses

BEING WITH PAIN

BEING WITH PASSIONS

BEING WITH HEART

Cultivate Compassion.

A GURU

A Teacher

A Creative
Man

A Wise
Man

A YOGI

A Man

A Fallible
Man

A Human

Expand your Awareness.

In the MiddLe
of ALL the Stuff...
Spot A PReCious
Moment.

A Beautiful
Pink Moment

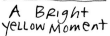

A Bright
Yellow Moment

A Deep
Blue Moment

A Small
Ray moment

A Mysterious
Green Moment

A Delicious
Red Moment

Honor every Moment.

Just
Listen.

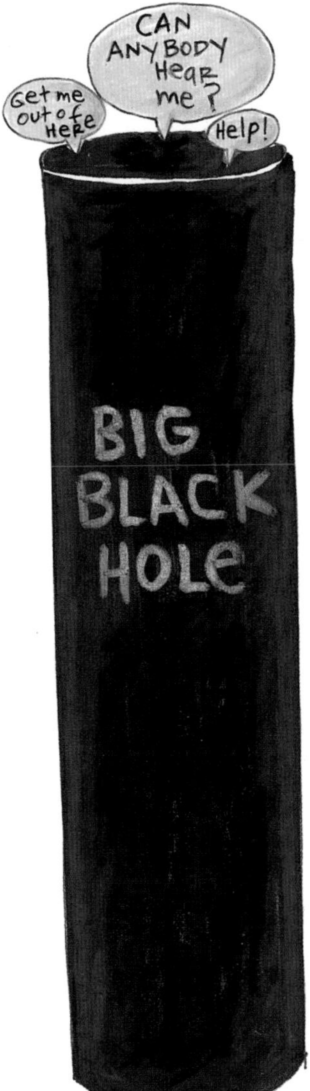
Get me out of HERE
CAN ANYBODY Hear me?
Help!
BIG BLACK HOLE

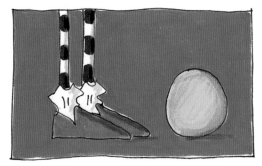

Act As if It's Nothing...

Act As if It's Something
To PLAY With...

Act As If It's Something
To get LOSt in...

Act As If It's Something
TO GO THROUGH.

ROOM TO BE CRAZY

ROOM TO CRY

ROOM TO CARE

ROOM TO BE SCARED

ROOM TO PANIC

ROOM TO Breathe

ROOM TO BE WEIRD

ROOM TO BE WILD

ROOM TO BE LOST

Make Room for What You Need.

Feeling
Secure...

I found
the Courage...

To Have
the Faith...

To Express
my Joy.

Open your Heart.

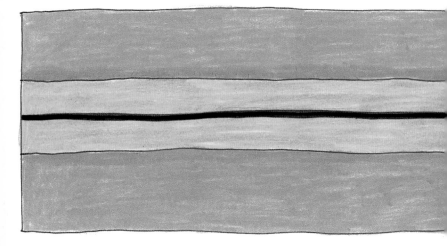

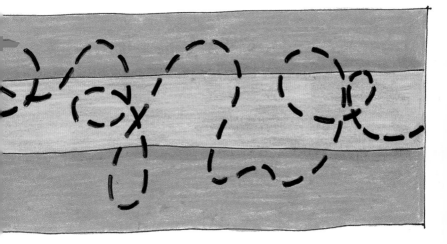

TRaveL the Road in YouR own way.

When you
Can't Decide...
Use Your Smile
as a Guide.

Explore Options.

Accept who you are
in this moment.

COLOR YOUR WORLD
With ALL that NOURishes
YOUR SOUL.

Anything
IS POSSIBLE
HERE.

EMPTY

SPACE

NOTHING

AVAILABLE

OPEN

BLANK

CLEAR

FREE

CHanging LabeLs
Changes PossibiLities.

Everything Happens
In Its own Time.

If what you're
Doing Isn't working...
DO Anything
Else.

IT'S OK TO NOT KNOW.

Practice Patience.

CRAZY Person
Going over
the Edge...

Rebellious
Person crossing
Boundaries...

CURIOUS
PERSON.
EXPLORING the
Unknown...

COURAGEOUS
PERSON Moving
Into NEW
TERRITORY

Seek New Perspectives.

Look up. Look Down.
Look ALL Around.

Signs of suffering...

Signs of well-being.

Notice
what Lifts
YOUR
Spirits.

Changing Context
Changes Experience.

THIS IS WHERE
I STRUGGLED.

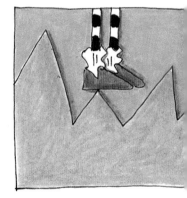

THIS IS WHERE
I LET GO.

THIS IS WHERE
I softened.

THIS IS WHERE
I KNOW.

Notice Sensations.

Sings in the
shower

cries at
movies

watches
sunsets

brushes
the dog

puffs the
pillows

gives
back rubs

offers .
free advice

makes tuna
sandwiches
on english
muffins

wraps
presents

CHERISHES
DESSERTS

Reads Stories
OUT LOUD

Takes
NaPS

GLUES
BROKEN PLATES

SmiLes

Hugs

ARRanges
FLOWERS

ReARRanges
Furniture

COLORS
OUTSide the
Lines

Acknowledge your Gifts.

CReate
YOUR own
ReaLity.

IT takes courage to step
into the Unknown.

Conversation

Dancing

Dreaming

♡

ⓖ

Wandering
Aimlessly   △   Singing

✗

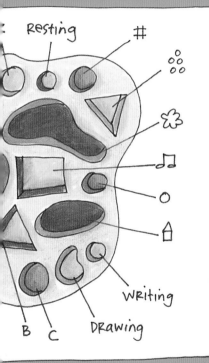

resting

\#

writing

Drawing

B   C

CARve ouT Space
foR what you VaLue.

one view

Another view

Many views

overview

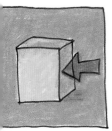

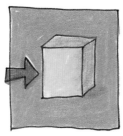

Right View

Opposing View

Scenic View

Re-view

Consider Another Point of view.

Notice
what makes
Sense
NOW.

THEN.

WHEN.

NOW.

Sometimes I'm
JUST A BLOB.

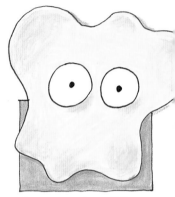

Sometimes I'm
A REALLY BIG BLOB.

Sometimes I'm A
DARK and MYSTERIOUS
BLOB.

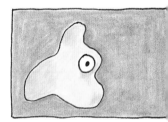

Sometimes I'm
ONLY PARTLY A
BLOB.

Sometimes I'm
A BLOB of FUN.

Sometimes I'm
A PERFECT BLOB.

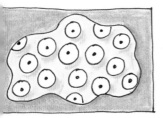

Sometimes I'm
An Insightful
BLOB.

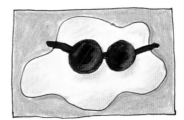

Sometimes I
Disguise
MY BLOBNESS.

Witness yourself.

If you work
with It...
It WILL WORK
for You.

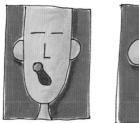

  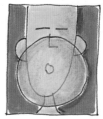

BeWARE of the DARK...

BeWARE of the Light...

If You choose the DARK... there is No Lig

  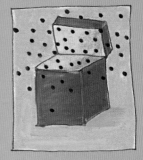

f you choose the Light...

What was Hidden ...

IS BRight.

Be willing to Feel the TRuth.

IT'S NOT WHat it IS...

It's How
You Relate
to It.

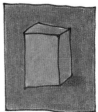

It's what
You compare
It to.

It's How (
can serve
You.

It's what
You can
Learn from
It.

It's YOUR
THoughts
About it.

It's the
Question
You ask
of It.

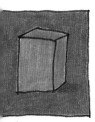

It's How it
Moves You.

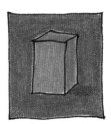

It's what
You Believe
About it.

It's How
You Use
It.

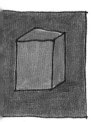

It's the
context
you put
it in.

It's what
It means
to You.

It's How
You Respond
to It.

The End is just the Beginning of Something Else.

Believe
in
MiracLes.

SAFe

cHALLenging

CeRTain